Wai Dan Gung

Hartmut von Czapski

Wai Dan Gung

Hartmut von Czapski

Fotos Ellen und Hartmut von Czapski

Impressum

Bibliographic information of the German National Library:

The German National Library records this publication in the German National Bibliography; detailed bibliographic data are available on the Internet via http://dnb.dnb.de.

© 2021 Hartmut von Czapski

Fotos Ellen und Hartmut von Czapski

Manufacture and publishing: BoD – Books on Demand, Norderstedt

ISBN: 9783753441856

Content:

Wai Dan Gung

The 20 "Exercises of the Outer Mercury"

are an ancient form of the Chinese Daoyin, today's qigong and go back to the Tang Dynasty (8th/9th century AD) .

Allegedly, in the following centuries, these exercises were only passed on to members of the imperial family.

This exercise series has a powerful and strengthening effect on all systems of body and mind, all meridians, all internal organs, muscles and tendons. In China, they say that you have to do a new exercise for 100 days to master it and feel the effect to its full. The 100 days are a symbolic period of time that can be longer or shorter depending on the ability of the practitioner.

Wai Dan Gong is considered a particularly effective form of Qi Gong, as it mobilizes and distributes the life energy Qi intensively in the body, so that a strengthening, positive effect begins early. Already after the first exercises you can feel tingling in the hands, arms and legs as a sign of increased blood circulation and care. The endpoints or starting points of the meridians are located at the finger and toe tips. Gentle strains activate them. There are vibrations that spread towards the body. As the exercise routine progresses, this is becoming more and more noticeable.

Wai Dan Gung is mainly found in Taiwan, Malaysia, Indonesia, Singapore, the Philippines, Thailand and Asian emigrants, also in America.

About the author

Hartmut von Czapski

Holistic practitioner since 1984. Since 1987 exercise of acupuncture (teacher Ms. Dr. Li Te, chief physician of the Nankei Clinic). Several stays in China with specialist training.

1987 Scientific education at the University. Tübingen passed: "Ecology and its biological foundations".

Since 1990 seminars, yoga and Qi Gong courses at various V.H.S. in the area. Among other things, 25 years of work at V.H.S. Wesel. Since 1990 well over 1000 Qi Gong lessons held.

Qi Gong Teacher 49009 of Mi Gong Rulai Buddhist Center for Qi Gong, Shanghai.

Trained as a Qi Gong therapist by Prof. Wu, Shanghai.

Lectures also for vitorgan and at Medica in Düsseldorf on the treatment of incontinence with T.C.M..
1999 Acupuncture training for dentists; Teacher activity at the HP School Dinslaken, courses on various therapies (homeopathy, discharge procedures, FRZM, etc.), also exam preparation courses.

Taught Qi Gong Forms:

Medical Qi Gong according to Prof.Wu.

Taiji-Qigong to Li Ding.

Ten meditations on the Wu Dang mountain.

The eighteenfold method of exercise.

The "movements of the 5 animals".

Qi Gong after Guo Lin for immune strengthening.

The "Eight Elegant Exercises."

"Wai Dan Gong"

Tai Chi for beginners according to Dr. JiangHao-quan.

And much more.

Qi Gong

The term "Qi Gong" includes various types of exercises to absorb the "Qi", the life energy, and to let it flow in the energy pathways, the so-called "meridians". It's a substance you normally don't see or touch, but you can feel. The old chin. Philosophers thought that Qi was an original substance that originated in the Big Bang.

After the chin. Med. Conception, Qi is a continuously moving and active substance, the basic substance from which the body arises. Qi receives the human life functions. According to the definition, Qi in qi gong is a "Essence" substance in the body with a certain energy. Qi can be formed, developed, transformed and moved in the body. Breathing moves the energy in the meridians. But even after a long practice of Qi Gong, you can move and absorb the Qi with the mind in the body.

These body and breathing exercises have a tradition of at least 4000 years in China, as can be seen from descriptions on grave goods. A distinction is made between different types of exercises. On the one hand, the soft Qi Gong, which contains many meditative elements based on the imagination and is often performed while sitting or lying down. On the other hand, we know the hard Qi Gong, which also strengthens the muscles and tendons and massages the internal organs. Consider, for example the performances of the Shaolin monks in Kung Fu or the acrobatic skills of the actors of the Peking Opera. But Qi Gong exercises not only strengthen the body, but also soothe the mind and regulate the vegetative nervous system.

A special form is the therapeutic Qi Gong, which prescribes certain exercises for certain diseases. Like any empirical science, Qi Gong is always evolving. In recent decades, for example certain new anti-cancer exercises have become famous for their good successes (Qi Gong after Guo Lin for immune strengthening). The Shanghai High Blood Pressure Research Institute has already published work in 1978 with reports on changes that Qi Gong is making in the ECG and EEG. Work has also been published on the fact that our sympathetic nervous system, which is overactive due to constant stress, achieves relaxation through Qi Gong by predominant parasympathetic.

In China, there is a department of traditional Chinese medicine in many hospitals, in addition to the Department of Conventional Medicine. This includes the treatment room for the Qi Gong therapist. Here, the patient is not only taught exercises that he should practice regularly at home, the therapist also encloses the patient with energy, which he himself has absorbed.
Training as a Qi Gong therapist is usually lengthy. After 5 years of practice, you can teach Qi Gong exercises, after 10 years you can also treat.
Mr. von Czapski has been trained by Prof. Wu Zhong Hu as a Qi Gong therapist.

Major energy centres

Hui Yen, KG1. In the middle of the dam, between anus and sex.

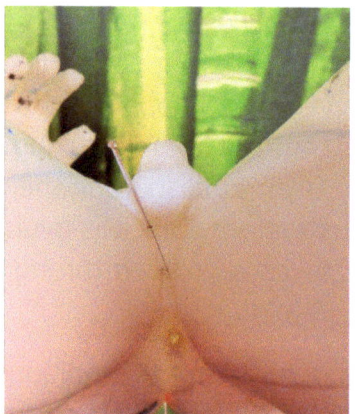

"Real" Dantian. Lies between the navel and the spine.

Lower dantian, about 2 cross fingers wide under the navel. About at the level of the acupuncture point"Qi Hai", Sea of Energy.

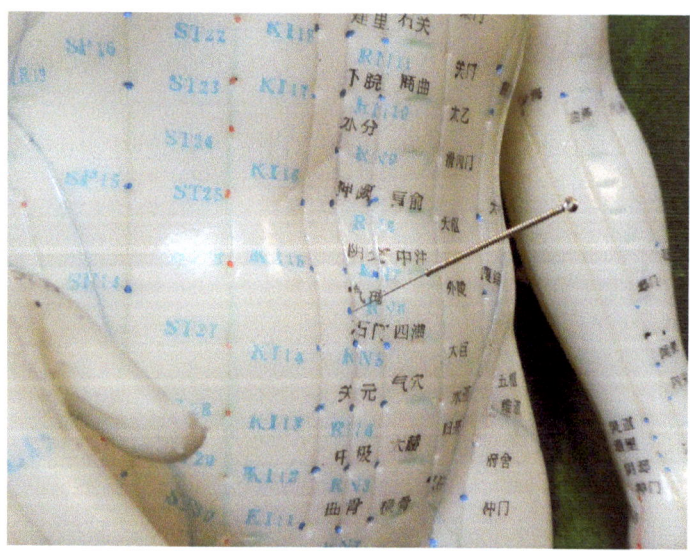

Middle Dantian, Heart Center. Tan Zhong.
At the height of a cowl on the sternum, between
the nipples.

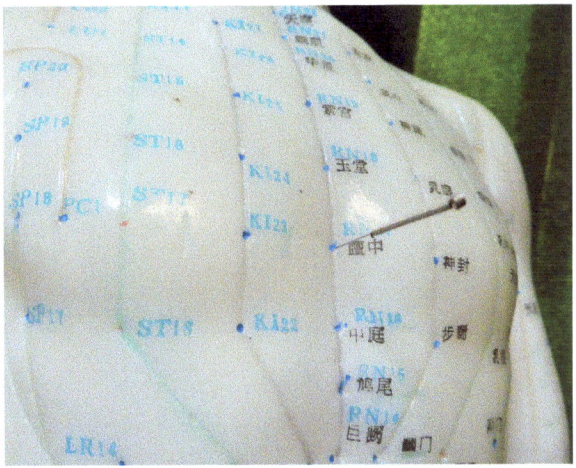

Upper Dantian, Yintang. Between the eyebrows, just
above the root of the nose.

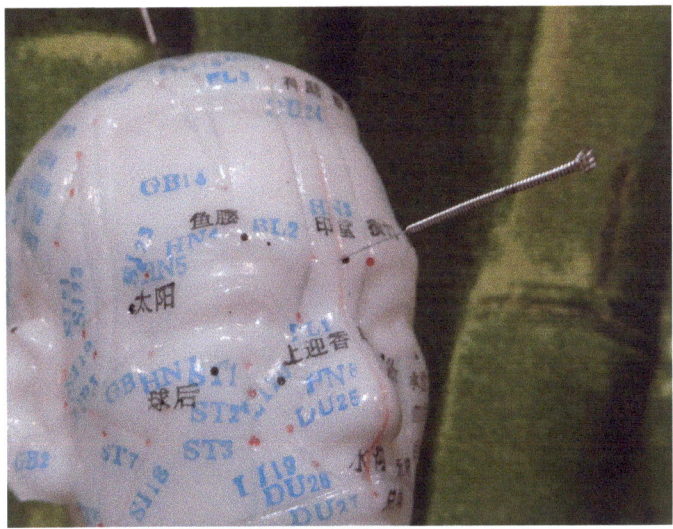

Energy uptake and delivery points

Yongchuan. When we "claw" the toes into the ground, a cowl is created below the base toe joints. Point kidney 1.

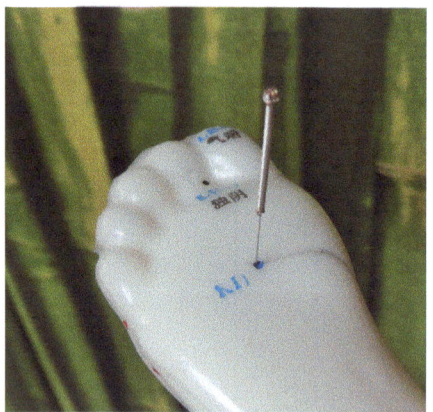

Laogong. When we tilt the fingertip of the ring finger into the palm of the hand, we get to this point.

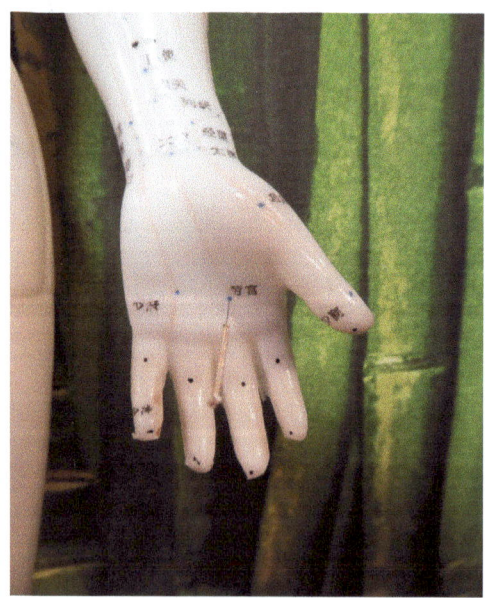

Basic position

Place your feet shoulder-width and parallel.

Bend your knees, but not beyond the tips of the feet.

Tilt the pelvis forward down so that the lumbar spine straightens. In people with a hollow back, this is often difficult at the beginning, the upper body tilts backwards. This should be straightened.

The spine should be as straight as possible.

The chin is slightly lowered, the cervical spine is stretched.

All nerve impulses can flow more freely.

Take back the shoulders, then let your arms hang loosely. Relax your shoulders. Move the elbows slightly to the side. This creates some space in the armpits.

The hands are not stretched, loose, but slightly stretched in the palms to absorb energy. Light, involuntary movements of the fingers are a good sign when absorbing energy.

We can imagine that the feet, like roots of a tree, reach into the depths. The torso is movable like the branches of a tree without giving up the basic position described above.
Try to come to rest, to absorb the nature and the life energy in it. For this purpose, the inner mindset should be like an empty white space.

The basic position should be taken before and possibly also between the exercises for 1-2 minutes in order to feel the effect.

In the basic state we breathe only through the nose, during the exercises we breathe in through the nose and breath out through the open mouth.

Since we open ourselves to the Qi of the environment at Qi Gong, we should not practice in strong winds (creates so-called "wind diseases"), on a tearing river (get the energy off us), before a thunderstorm (puts us under tension) or in fever (is increased). In the case of a coronary heart disease practice in consultation with the teacher.

1) Embrace the moon

Place your feet next to each other. The feet turn outwards so that the feet point forward and stand in a line. The mouth is closed, the tongue is behind the upper row of teeth, this creates a connection between 2 meridians, the "Great Governeur" (rear center line) and the "Little Governeur" (front center line). The hands lie under the navel on top of each other, the left over the right, the thumb tips touch each other. Breathe vigorously and move your hands up in a circular direction. We look up. The energy rises from the dantian upwards.
We stay in this position for two/three seconds at full inhalation.
Exhale vigorously through the open mouth and lower the hands and put them on top of each other again in front of the lower abdomen. The energy sinks back into the Dantian.
Repeat 3 x.

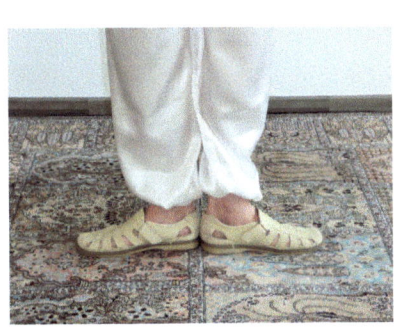

2) Turn the Head

Place your feet next to each other. The feet turn outwards so that the feet point forward and stand in a line.
Breathing is calm and fluid.
We raise both arms sideways horizontally upwards and stretch our fingers upwards, towards the head, the elbows remain stretched. We look at the right middle finger and count slowly to 20.
After some practice we feel the Qi energy there with a tingling or trembling.
Then we turn the look at the left middle finger and count slowly to 20 and try to feel Qi there as well.

24

3) Walk on ice

Place the feet slightly more than shoulder-width. Put your hands on top of Dantian. The right over the left in men, the left over the right in women.
With the strong inhalation, push the left foot forward obliquely, do not lift the foot and put it on the tip of the toe. At the same time, bend the upper body slightly forward from the hip. Both hands press on the belly, the energy rises from the dantian upwards.
With the exhalation, reset the foot, leave the abdomen loose, raise the upper body, the energy decreases from the back to the lower abdomen.
Repeat the exercise on the other side.
Repeat the whole exercise 3 times.

4) Raising your arm

Light burrows, both arms straight forward, the palms facing each other. Inhale.
Throw both arms backwards, look at the left hand and exhale with your mouth open.
Inhale and guide hands forward again.
Repeat 3 times.
Hold both arms up and slowly count to 30. Pay attention to tingling or movements in the finger. Repeat the same movements, looking to the right side.

5) Hold the basket

With legs apart, light squats. Direct your arms forward, as if you were grasping a large basket. Do not raise the elbows. The fingertips at sun braid height, below the sternum.
Turn the upper body right and left from the hip. Keep your torso straight and relaxed. The weight stays in the middle, the feet firmly on the floor. Inhale on one side, exhale on the other.
Repeat 9 times.

6) Bend the trunk

Wide straddle. Loose fists. Thumbs up. Inhale through the nose, bend forward and exhale vigorously through the open mouth. Left, open hand to left foot, right fist to right knee. Knee stretched, look forward. Breathe again when straightening up. Repeat on the other side. 3 x right and 3 x left.

7) Harvesting rice

Light straddle, loose fists, thumbs facing forward. Exhale, bend forward, knees loose. The hands open and touch the top of the feet with their fingertips. Breathe in.
Put your left foot a little bit to the left and then stretch the left hand up to the left, face to the outside. The upper body tilts to the left. Exhale. At the end of the exhalation, stretch the right hand to the bottom right and thus straighten the body again.
Go back to the starting position and repeat the exercise on the other side. 3 x left and 3 x right.

8) Bending your back

Light staddle, knees loose, pelvis tilted forward. Loose fists. Exhale.
With the deep inhalation, open your hands and guide you forward, up and backward in a circular arc. Bend the torso backwards. The energy rises from the lower abdomen (dantian) upwards. Look at your hands. With the exhalation through the mouth, guide the hands forward to the horizontal, straighten up the upper body again.
Knee loose, relax. The energy sinks back into the lower abdomen.
Bend back with the next inhalation, etc.
Bend backwards 3 times.

9) Seeking relaxation

Basic position. We let the breathing flow calmly.
First, focus on the apex point "Bai Hui". As if we were hanging by a silk thread there. Then we focus on our hands. They are loose, except for the middle fingers. We stretch them towards the ground. After a while we feel a tingling, trembling or swinging in our hands. If the swinging in the arms does not set itself, we can help gently. The Qi raises the arms up and after a lot of practice we can steer the Qi to where it is needed.

10) Breath like a turtle

The turtle is a symbol of long life. Basic position. Put both hands on the point Dantian. The women's right hand first, men's left hand first. Both palms on top of each other. Stretch the chin a little. With the inhalation through the nose, the torso bendback, the abdomen slightly bulging (abdominal breathing), the chin pullback, look forward. The anus is attracted so that the energy rises upwards, from Hui Yin to Bai Hui. When exhaling through the open mouth, bend forward and stretch chin forward. Relax the anus. The energy decreases downwards.

Inhalation and exhalation should be the same length. At the beginning, count up to 10 seconds and extend the breathing phases up to 20-30 seconds with continuous practice.
9 times inhalation and exhalation.
Then leave your hands on Dantian for 1-2 minutes and track down the base position.

11) Swinging your arms

Basic position, but slightly wider and deeper.

Press the point Di.4 "Hou Kou" 10 seconds with the right hand edge. Then press the right point between the thumb and index finger with the left edge of the hand. Inhale and bend the torso forward, push the knees, stretch the arms backwards on the sides of the body, the palms upwards.

Exhale and swing your arms forward. The knees swing loosely, the upper body straightens up.

9 times back and forth.

Bend forward again, arms on the body, palms upwards. Then stretch your hands 36 times down. Waiting if you feel a tingling or swinging in your fingers, hands or arms. Then swing forward, straighten up, stretch arms forward, palms down. Then stretch your fingers to the body 36 times. Waiting if you feel a tingling or swinging in your fingers, hands or arms.

12) Swinging the wings

Basic position. Raise toes. Stretch both arms forward, palms against each other. Stretch out hands on both sides, palms up. Keep shoulders as relaxed as possible. Stretch your fingers 36 times down. Waiting if you feel a tingling or swinging in your fingers, hands or arms.
You can also help the swinging of the arms a little bit.

13) Fist circles

Basic position. Normal breathing. Raise both arms sideways and hold the fists in front of your ears. The thumbs are in the fists, the inside of the fist points forward. Now the fists 36 times powerfully clench together. Shoulders and upper arms remain relaxed.

Then wait until the fists in front of the ears begin to circle. You can also help if it doesn't happen on its own. The movement can also reproduce into the arms.

14) Balancing Heaven and Earth

Basic position. Holding an imaginary ball in front of your body, for example the right hand at heart level, facing down. The left hand on Dantian height, facing upwards.

We now raise our right hand upwards, the gaze follows the hand. The palm facing upwards, the fingers pointing to the center.

The left hand moves downwards next to the body, fingertips facing forward. Stretch both elbows as far as possible.

Now stretch the upper hand 36 times to the head, the lower hand stretches up 36 times at the same time. Then look forward again. Waiting if you feel a tingling or swinging in your fingers, hands or arms.

Now perform the same exercise sideways.

15) Crossing your arms

Basic status. Cross your arms in front of your chest. The palms point outwards and are vertical on the nipples. Now stretch your hands 36 times. Then remove the tension from the hands and wait for slight movements, or tingling, of the finger.

Then change arms and cross and repeat the exercise.

16) Presenting the pearl

The feet are positioned slightly wider than shoulder-width. Place on the tip of your toes. Place your hands in front of the lower abdomen, the palms up. Push the elbows forward a little. The fingertips point against each other, at the level of the energy center Dantian. Turn your head 3 times to the right and to the left. Breathe in to the side, exhale forward.
Then bend your fingers 36 times down. Remove the tension from the hands and wait for slight movements, or tingling, of the finger. If this does not happen by itself at the beginning, you can also help a little..
Move your hands from Dantian to Tanzhong, inhale. From Tanzhong to Dantian lower and exhale. Leave your shoulders loose. 9 times. Lower the feet, return to the base.
The energy is moved up and down on the Meridian "Little Governor". In addition, the exercise strengthens kidney energy, our main life energy.

17) Turn the fuselage

Base stand, then place the feet slightly wider than shoulder width. Direct the palms down at the Dantian level. The fingertips point against each other with 4 fingers wide distance. Push the elbows slightly forward so that the hands and forearms are on a line. Stretch your hands 36 times upwards.

Then turn the pelvis up to 36 times to the left and right. The upper body and arms remain in the position, are only moved by the movement of the pelvis. The weight remains in the middle. Stay loose in your knees.

Forward, stop and focus on your fingers. Waiting for slight movements, or tingling, the finger.

The energy is moved on the special meridian "belt meridian". It promotes the energy of the abdominal organs and causes a balance from above and below.

18)Strengthening yourself

Basic position, feet slightly more than shoulder width. Move your arms forward. Direct the palms forward, not above shoulder height. Stretch your hands to the body 36 times, point your palms forward in a relaxed manner.
The toes dig easily into the ground. Check the base again and again, so pelvis tilted forward, knees loose, shoulders relax. Wait. Tingling or involuntary movements can spread along the arms or along the legs towards the body. The points "Yongchuan" under the soles of the feet and "Laogong" in the palms are activated.

19) Swing your feet

Stretch both arms slightly to the side of the body, directing palms to the back. Fold the index finger, middle finger and ring finger, but not the thumbs and small fingers. Place weight on the right leg, push through knees, stretch left leg obliquely forward, the tip of the foot hangs in the air. Now stretch your foot to the body 36 times. In this position, wait for a tingling or involuntary movement of the foot or leg. Leave shoulders loose.

Then stretch the leg diagonally backwards and stretch the foot again 36 times. In this position, wait for a tingling or involuntary movement of the foot or leg.

Repeat the exercise on the other side.

The energy flows through the leg and the point "Hui Yin" into the lower body and its organs. There can be a feeling of warmth there.

20) Walk like a crane

Place feet wider than shoulder width. Kneel down a little bit.
Raise your arms a little bit on the side. Palm facing
backwards, stretching index and middle fingers.
Raise one leg, leave it loose from the knee down, inhale,
tighten anus.
Step forward, foot, gently like a feather, put on, exhale and
relax anus.
7 steps forward.
7 steps backwards, turning your hands around, so hand areas
are directed forwards.
3 times forward and backward.
Finally, stay in the basic position for at least 2 minutes. Then
go around a bit and loosen arms and legs.

Qi Gong Books from Hartmut von Czapski
Qi Gong sitting
ISBN 9783750424692 English ISBN: 9783750431409

In this book 34 Qi Gong exercises are described which are performed while sitting. From simple exercise exercises to Tuina massage exercises, breathing exercises and concentration exercises. These exercises improve energy absorption, strengthen self-healing powers and balance the vegetative nervous system. They promote the ability to concentrate and inner peace. They have a positive effect on the digestive organs, muscles, tendons, joints and spine. The increased oxygen uptake strengthens the heart and lungs.

It is very suitable as an exercise book for occupational medicine, for nursing homes, as a graduation for each Qi Gong course or simply for all office or computer workers in between.

The many photos and the clear description make it easy to understand the exercises.

Taiji Qi Gong
ISBN 9783749469413 Engl.ISBN:9783752820072

This book describes 22 Taiji Qi Gong exercises. These exercises improve energy absorption, strengthen the self-healing powers and compensate for the vegetative nervous system. They promote the ability to concentrate and inner calm. They have a positive effect on the digestive organs, the muscles, the tendons, joints and the spine. The increased oxygen uptake strengthens the heart and lungs.

Qi Gong Stand Exercises

ISBN 9783744809665 Engl.ISBN: 9783751907323

In this book 23 Qi Gong stand exercises are described. These exercises improve energy absorption, strengthen self-healing powers and balance the vegetative nervous system. They promote concentration and inner calm. They strengthen the muscles and tendons. The standing positions of the 5 animals (monkey, deer, bear, tiger, crane) are also suitable for children.

Medical Qi Gong according to Prof. Wu

ISBN 9783744829427 Engl. ISBN: 9783751904575

In this book, exercises are shown which show an excellent effect on the following symptoms: high and low blood pressure, stomach and intestinal problems, lung problems, insomnia, nervousness, lack of concentration, energylessness, back pain and excessive stress.

With regular and persistent exercise of the Qi Gong, the practitioner can improve his or her health and and find relaxation.

Since the exercises can be carried out with different effort, they are also suitable for older, weakened people.

Tai Hu Lake Qi Gong

ISBN: 9783750494091 English ISBN: 9783751916479

This series of exercises originated in the song dynasty. In the vicinity of Tai Hu Lake, these exercises were developed and later modified.

The energy absorption is stimulated, the muscles strengthened, the mobility improves, the blood circulation of the internal organs and the oxygen uptake are increased. The imitation of the animal movements and the movements of a sea-dweller stimulates the imagination of children and also provide cheerfulness in adults.

You don't have to do the whole exercise series, you can also take out individual exercises for your daily exercise program.

Each book costs 12,-€. The books are available in any bookstore or on the Internet on Amazon or at www.bod.de. A small preview is also possible there. Each book costs 12,-€. Also available as an e-book.